To: Katie

From: Hope

This book is dedicated to all the dogs
I have had the great joy to share my life
with. To those who I have rescued . . .
and to each who has rescued my heart
with their unconditional love. It is their
"secrets" that I am able to now share.

—J. W.

Illustrations copyright © 2008 Jody Wright

Designed by Heather Zschock

Copyright © 2008
Peter Pauper Press, Inc.
202 Mamaroneck Avenue
White Plains, NY 10601
All rights reserved
ISBN 978-1-59359-895-2
Printed in China
7 6 5 4

Visit us at www.peterpauper.com

50 Secrets
HUMANS
Should Know

Secrets...

Come closer. Listen carefully. The thing about secrets that makes them simply irresistible is that they are hidden treasures just beyond the surface.

When I wrote *50 Secrets Humans Should Know* I found I was on a voyage of discovery that had started as a toddler with my first puppy. Each step I took in learning to walk was a step with a loyal companion animal into the realm of spirit.

Today, I am left wondering whether the great secrets in our lives are revealed from the work of great geniuses or revolutionary rocket scientists, or from the unconditional love of a wagging tail, the lick of a  wet tongue, and the constant reassurance of a four-legged friend.

Perhaps these creatures hold secrets available to anyone who wants to take a closer look inward (which, of course, is NO SECRET to those who have shared their lives with a companion animal).

In the pages that follow, you'll get to experience the secrets these beautiful creatures have shared through their play, actions, soulful looks and "in-the-moment" living. May their spirits always whisper their sweet secrets to you as well!

PLAY IS GENIUS!

Albert Einstein once said, "Imagination is a preview of life's coming attractions." Dogs have always known this somehow. They are GENIUSES BY INSTINCT. Watch your "best friend" and it's easy to see that, through his eyes, there is a world of friends who want to do nothing more than wiggle, wag, and romp. So imagine a friendly universe and see how much better the day becomes.

LOOK DEEPER

See past the outside "stuff" and stare deeply into the part of each soul to the place that really matters! Often, "looking deeper" finds that ever-flowing well of irrepressible, renewable LOVE.

DO WHAT YOU LOVE!

We all have to work at boring jobs and put our dreams on hold, right? It doesn't have to be that way. Become a master at getting what the spirit needs. Find ways, each and every day, to DO WHAT YOU TRULY LOVE.

STAY CURIOUS

EXPLORE, climb to greater heights and go see what's on the other side. Staying curious may not give us nine lives but it certainly makes this one nine times more fun!

BE ALL EARS

There's a fine art to **LISTENING.** Don't let it be a lost art.

WHEN PUGNACIOUS, BE GRACIOUS

At times, life calls for us to be aggressive. We are pugnacious. Being gracious is a THOUGHTFUL COUNTERBALANCE.

EXPERIENCE WONDER

Rediscover the SENSE OF WONDER.
There are still so many adventures yet to be pursued for each of us.

FIND BEAUTY

Each day find time for beauty. Rediscover the riches to be found in a simple flower, the laughter of a child, or THE SETTING SUN.

BE INTENSE

Being intense is not a bad thing. BE INTENSELY HAPPY...

or interesting ... or funny. Step away from the lukewarm. Experience passion.

SAVOR SWEET DREAMS

If you DARE TO, DREAM. It isn't always safe to go where you haven't been before. Sometimes there are nightmares. Yet there are also sweet ecstasies, moments of hyper-awareness, and insights into worlds that are found nowhere else but in the back of one's eyelids.

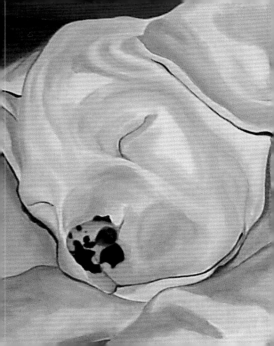

BE TRUE BLUE

Being "true blue" is something that should be HIGHLY rated. It means that you can be counted on when other colors fade.

THERE IS POWER IN INTENTION

There are many times when you must pick a firm direction, set a path, and stick with it. Trust in your powerful GIFT OF INTENTION.

BE IRRESISTIBLE

You know you are!
It's OK to explore
being IRRESISTIBLE
on occasion.
It invites people in.

MAINTAIN PEACE

Keep an open mind and MAINTAIN YOUR PEACE—even when things seem a bit chaotic. Problems often dissolve, creative solutions emerge, and if nothing else, the world looks like a better place!

Original Paintings

The illustrations in this book were created from
Jody Wright's paintings on original canvases.
Jody creates paintings using acrylics. She works
from photographs of the dogs, many of whom are
residing at shelters. She finds out about their per-
sonality and then selects the colors that will best
describe the "inner beauty" she sees. She also
accepts commissions from dog owners nationwide
so owners with dogs that have "forever homes"
also have "forever portraits" of their best friends.
"I don't try to tell a story by placing the dogs in
environments. For me, it's all about the spirit, and
when I look into those eyes I see a world of colorful
emotions," the artist says. "Those faces say it all!"
To see more of the artist's work and for a complete
listing of the galleries who represent her, please visit
the artist's website at:

www.wsggallery.com

e-mail: jody@wsggallery.com

RYAN (which means "little king") is a recently adopted chocolate Lab mix who challenges, provides inspiration, and is always ready to both give and receive unconditional love. Alas, not much is known about Ryan's background. He was dumped out in a rural town in West Virginia where a kind man cared for him in hopes that his owner would show up and reclaim him. When that didn't happen, and colder weather was in the forecast, the man turned him over to a local animal shelter. Later, a golden retriever rescuer took him in to help out the over-crowded shelter. Today, Ryan's future is bright . . . and so is he!

THUNDER

appeared at the artist's back door during a horrific thunderstorm. He was only four months old.

ZEBBIE followed the artist home when it was 10 degrees below zero outside. He prefers WARM, soft couches, meals with meat, and has only one drawback. He doubts the judgment of most humans.

About the Artist

I have the great pleasure in life to make a living as an artist who paints companion animals. In my work, I illustrate the incredible spirits within animals. I want people to stop and think, *"Look at this extraordinary spirit that just happens to be in the body of a dog or cat."*

With bold colors (usually not found in nature), I encourage the observer to take a closer look at what is often considered the *ordinary*.

I convey what is beneath the outside parameters and inward to the heart and soul. My work focuses on companion animals, many of whom are from shelters and are awaiting adoption. I donate a portion of the profits from my sales to help support animal adoption centers nationwide.

It is companion animals' beauty and how they experience life that continues to inspire me. Dogs reveal their colorful expressions of unconditional love & joy in this tribute to companion animals everywhere.

May their colorful spirits always brighten your day!

THERE ARE STILL NEW WORLDS TO DISCOVER

No matter how old we become, how many times we try and don't succeed, or love without having it returned, remember THERE ARE WORLDS YET TO BE DISCOVERED!

HAVE A SAFE PLACE

Each of us needs a sanctuary; a soft place to go when life seems too hard. Create safe places where you can retreat and RENEW YOUR SPIRIT.

IT'S THE LITTLE THINGS

When you have a task before you, attack the small things first. Work up to the larger projects with A SENSE OF ACCOMPLISHMENT.

BE LOYAL

Stand up for
someone,
watch their back,
or support them
in some way.
Loyalty is a way
to show people
you CARE DEEPLY.

REMEMBER YOUR "FIRSTS"

Cherish those "firsts" in your life that give it flavor. A FIRST KISS, a first glance, a first date, a first child ...
It's important to remember your firsts before you reach your lasts.

PROTECT WHAT'S IMPORTANT

Guard what is dear. Gather it close to the heart. Choose to KEEP IT SAFE.

EMBRACE SURPRISE

Surprise is the spice
that makes life
more tasty.
It takes a bland day
and transforms
it into something
EXTRAORDINARY.

IF THE WORLD IS GOING TO THE DOGS, REJOICE!

Romp in some water on a hot summer's afternoon, or play with a hose on those awful "dog days." Find something cool to sit on. FEEL THE GRASS between your toes. Let your world "go to the dogs" and see if your spirit doesn't thank you!

HANG OUT

Do absolutely nothing.
JUST HANG OUT.
A small still voice
is audible only
when we are able
to be silent enough
to hear it.

WAIT WHEN NECESSARY

But ONLY when it's necessary.
Life's too short to be constantly waiting for something to happen.
Set goals.
TAKE ACTION.

QUESTION THINGS

There is great freedom in asking questions and GREAT JOY in discovering the answers.

DREAM BIG

What is the point of
dreaming small?
If you attain something,
it won't be of any value
to you. SO DREAM BIG.
It won't always work out,
but you'll be able to
walk a little taller for
having tried.

CREATE EXCITEMENT

Find the POWER WITHIN to create excitement. Approach your life with an enthusiastic rhythm.

SEE FROM THE INSIDE OUT

Some of the most unique and INGENIOUS MINDS can be hiding in oddly packaged presentations.

GET TO THE POINT

All too often, we don't really get to THE HEART OF THE MATTER. Say what is important. Bring it out into the open.

SAY YES MORE

SAY YES. Not "maybe." Not "we'll see." Make "yes" a forthright, no-nonsense, formidable commitment.

HAVE A BALL

Why be so serious?
Remember that life
comes with an
expiration date.
GO HAVE A BALL!

TREAT YOURSELF LIKE A KING! (or QUEEN)

PAMPER YOURSELF on a day that isn't set aside for such things.
(This is especially true on those days when no one else truly understands your lordship!)

SHOW YOUR TRUE COLORS

Your INNER COMPASS knows which direction to point. Never be afraid to let your true colors show through.

GO WILD

There are times to play it safe and also plenty of times to go wild. Assess your risks wisely but don't leave out the WILD side.

OBSERVE CAREFULLY

Observe the source
of a tear, the fear
behind anger,
and the melancholy
of a moment lost.
TRUE SEEING
comes only from
careful observation.

LIVE LARGE

If you know you were meant to live large, don't let outside appearances fool you. BE LARGE from the inside out.

REPEAT YOURSELF

Go ahead and
BE REDUNDANT
every once in a while.
Sometimes good
things are worth
repeating.

WATCH FOR OPPORTUNITY

Be awake.
BE READY.
Opportunity appears
to us all but waits
around for no one.

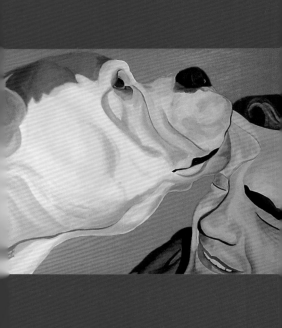

KISS MORE

As our life nears the final stretch, let it not be said that we didn't kiss enough. Don't be afraid to SHOW YOUR LOVE.

GET TO THE HEART & SOUL

Humans are often like layers of an onion. It doesn't have to be so complicated. Simply get to the heart and soul. FORGET THE LAYERS. Show those you love just how much you care!

BE GOLDEN

Within each of us is the ability to be "golden." Each of us shines in a way that makes the world just A LITTLE BIT BRIGHTER.

TREASURE YOUR FRIENDS

Friends are what you need most on your journey. Greet them with the joy they deserve and treasure them with KIND ACTIONS.

RACE TO LOVE

Race your life away—
but only when
it's toward LOVE,
JOY, and
HAPPINESS.

INDULGE IN NAPS

Humans should come with a "reset" button. But since they don't, it's ALWAYS A GOOD IDEA to do it manually. Indulge in a nap. It's amazing what it can do for one's perspective.

HUNT FOR LOVE

Some people say that man is suffering because the innate need to hunt and gather can't be satisfied in the civilized world. Why not HUNT FOR LOVE then? Gather as much as you want.

BE CHAIRMAN OF THE BORED

Contrary to popular belief, boredom is not fatal. Choose a day of boredom and you'll come back to your life with RENEWED EXUBERANCE!

LAUGH MORE!

Stretch your face. Smile. LAUGH. Consider it "facial calisthenics"!

DISCOVER INFINITE POSSIBILITIES

Infinite possibilities exist. Peer into a new environment and see what you can EXPERIENCE!

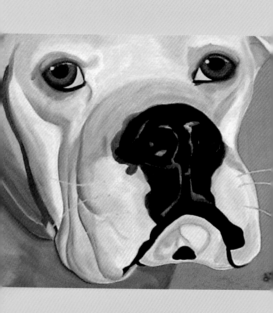

TREASURE BEING UNIQUE

There is nobody on earth who's exactly like you! Celebrate that refreshing ONE-OF-A-KIND status.

KEEP LOOKING UP

There is always enough time to face the floor in one's life. Choose to look up and you'll discover a WONDERFUL new view.